I0482300

Internet Marketing

10 Best Strategies to Become Marketing Guru and Earn More!

By:
James Stevens

Table of Contents

Introduction

Would you like to move from an internet marketing newbie to a guru in just a few days? It may seem difficult at first glance but it can be done if you are willing to apply amazing marketing strategies that have helped internet marketers in the past and today.

Internet marketing is advancing rapidly these days as many people are shifting their focus to this kind of marketing strategy. This comes down to consumers and their behavior, which has also changed. Chances of making a big name out of yourself are high with a basic understanding of internet marketing, but you should strive to become the guru that everyone is talking about! For this to happen, you must have a strategy in place.

Is it not better to be a trend setter than someone that is just following the masses? You have to work on your marketing strategies to achieve this and more. You need to be the creator, because this is what will empower you more and make you stand higher than everyone else in the internet marketing arena.

This eBook has great strategies that will help you elevate yourself and your product or service in internet marketing. This way, you shall be able to sell more, connect to your target market and help you build a business that enhances the lives of so many people.

Chapter 1:
Starting Out with Internet Marketing

Internet marketing is essential in this digital era. A decade ago, it was a strategy that received minimal attention, as companies continued to battle for space on traditional marketing platforms. Now, a lot of people search for what they want to buy on the internet therefore it is becoming necessary for business people to market their brands online in order to meet customer needs. The internet has therefore become the best platform to market whatever products or services that you are dealing with.

Internet marketing has various aims, the most prominent being attracting buyers to your website. You have to design your website in such a manner that it will attract as many potential buyers as possible. Provide content about the products or services that you are dealing with and provide information that potential buyers might be interested in so as to catch their attention. With internet marketing, you stand to gain more clients for your products or services, which interprets to more sales.

Beginning your journey in internet market is not a simple thing at all, but with a proper plan and the right guidance, you can easily become a great internet marketing guru.

Become an Internet Marketing Guru

The strategies that are contained within this book are meant to elevate you to internet marketing guru status. For that reasons, you need to understand what an internet marketing guru is.

The internet marketing guru has one main skill that they begin with. This is the ability to create and start a venture on the internet, and to build that venture through creative internet marketing growth strategies.

An internet marketing guru has the ability to look at the various marketing platforms that are available on the internet, and determine a way that they can work together to ensure profitability. For example, to increase presence, you can start by creating a blog that contains quality content, link this blog with a page on social media, and then use keyword research to ensure that you have the right words on your site to drive traffic.

Internet marketers connect with their customers directly, enabling them to act quickly on first-hand information for development of their products and services. An Internet Marketing guru will capitalize on these customers and work closely with them to attain results.

A marketing guru is a leader in his own market. He is the person people are looking out for in order to learn a few things about internet marketing for them to succeed in their own market. This person works with newbies and other internet marketers that want to attain success online. His name is all over the internet, all thanks to his great skills and hard work. He is enjoying great benefits which includes a good pay from all his efforts.

Chapter 2:
Why It's Important

In the beginning, only a few, top-rated companies used to get on with internet marketing but things have changed so much these days. All manner of businesses, whether small or large are now making use of internet marketing in order to enjoy the amazing benefits that it comes with. The technicality of internet marketing and the costs have reduced so much and today, anyone can afford to promote their business online, not just the businesses which are already doing well. This means that any business person can now enjoy the benefits if increased sales and other benefits that come with web marketing. Today, everything that is being done occurs easily over the internet. People of all ages are more attached to the internet. This is the reason why online marketing is the best way to market your business if you want to reach out to more people. Here are some benefits that you get to enjoy:

1. Your products or services will get a broad and global reach- The days when business people only sold to the people within their businesses are now gone. Online businesses are selling far and wide and internet marketing is helping create awareness of the existence of their products or services to those places where they cannot physically reach. Since many people are shopping online today, they are able to see products and services of companies that are both close home and those that are far in order to make the best choice of what they really want to buy.

2. Online marketing is highly flexible to multitasking- There is no better way to serve many clients at the same time and ensure that they are well satisfied than

through the internet. Online marketing will help you meet and interact with so many customers and consumers online and each of them will be well attended to, without fail. You do not have to increase the number of your employees in order to serve and interact with your clients better online, because this is very easy even when you have just a few online marketers for your business.

3. Internet marketing remains relevant so many years after the marketing period. The content in your website for instance will remain the same and people can get to know what you deal with a long time after you have set up your website. If you have an eBook for your products or services for instance, it will be read by many people even years after its launching and people will continue to learn about your existence way after the marketing period. Marketing period is therefore not limited and the promotion can continue to yield results for a long time.

4. This is the kind of marketing that runs round the clock without any additional costs. Once you start online campaigns for your brand, the campaign will continue running day and night, even on public holidays and over the weekends. Good thing is that you do not pay more for that, not even overtime payments for your staff.

5. Internet marketing is cost effective- To start with, you do not need any initial capital to start an online campaign for your goods or services. You can start with blog marketing, email marketing and social media marketing at a much lower cost than what you would pay for other marketing strategies. You do not need to

pay your staff so much money for online marketing too; as soon as the website is up and running, things will fall in place without anyone doing so much work to drive in traffic.

6. It will save time for your business- Web marketing is very easy and fast to start. You do not need to plan a lot about the right time to launch the campaign because any time that is convenient for you is good enough. If you want to start email marketing campaign, setting it up can be done in just a few hours and in just a few minutes, the auto-responder will be on and you will be ready to start marketing as much as you can.

Chapter 3:
The First Two Strategies –
Determine your Reach

The next few chapters are all about getting to the heart of the matter of internet marketing. They include details on strategies that have been tried, tested and found to be successful. This chapter addresses your reach as an internet marketer and attaining success.

Go mobile

The internet is no longer limited to the personal computer as it was a decade ago. More people access the internet using mobile devices than they do on traditional PCs. Therefore, you must ensure that any marketing efforts you make are optimized for mobile phones devices.

This means that using a mobile device, you should be able to easily search for and gain access to the website that is selling a product. Furthermore, scrolling through the products should be done with ease, and one should be able to use a shopping cart to complete a transaction.

Mobile devices now offer mobile banking platforms which allow for easier connection and withdrawals from bank accounts. When making a purchase, having tools in place that facilitate faster conclusion of a sale will mean that the customer enjoys more convenience. This is something that an internet marketer can capitalize on.

Emphasize mobile optimization for your website. Design your website in such a manner that people on mobile devices can access everything that you have on your website on their small screens. Some of the changes you will have to include on your website include:

- Making it smaller in size for mobile devices

- Reducing the details so that when on a mobile device there is focus on key points. Expandable menus are an ideal solution.

- Use of larger navigation buttons

- Include fewer graphics

- Include a phone contact that starts a call when clicked

The power of mobile ubiquity cannot be underestimated. Look around and see just how many people are using mobile devices today. You have a great chance to make it in internet marketing through mobile marketing.

A major benefit that you will enjoy with this is that mobile will bring you closer to your market and it will spread your market reach. It is in fact the best connection to establish with your potential clients since many people are on their mobile devices too, not just those who are using smart phones. This also increases your market range in that you can reach out to more people through their mobile devices. With your employees on mobile as well, you can be sure that service to your clients will be more efficient and effective, which works to keep you in operation for a longer time.

Use Videos

YouTube is becoming a very popular platform today Whereas in the past it was all about playing videos for the purposes of entertainment, advertisers have found creative ways of incorporating their marketing messages into the videos. This has resulted in higher conversions and creating more awareness with ease. YouTube has about 800 million visitors every month, which means that you can find an excellent segment to target if you want to make your brand stand out from the rest. YouTube can therefore help you in internet marketing through video marketing as the main strategy to introduce YouTube visitors to your brand, products and services. Just imagine how many people watch YouTube videos every day and imagine how much you can accomplish if they like what you are selling.

There are several ways that you can use YouTube. First, you can create marketing videos which you establish on your very own YouTube channel. These are best for demonstrating your expertise, and giving instructions on the best way to use your products. You can also create videos of customer testimonials which reveal how successful your product or service has been in the past. The videos should have such elements as a headline that has a popular and easy to search keyword, a simple but very clear message to your target market and a call to action. Let them know how easily they can reach you or what they can do, for instance to subscribe to your channel or to visit your website for more information. Ensure that the quality of the video is top notch to attract more viewers. This should work really well in your favor.

Use of videos come with a few benefits to the business:

- Video adds the "wow" cause to your web marketing. Videos are eye catching and also very effective. They add a punch to your internet marketing because they stimulate viewers more than word or images can. It is easy to remember something that has been conveyed through a video, which makes it a more effective strategy to use in your marketing campaign.

- Video puts a face to your brand- in as much as you can explain to your prospects what you are and what you have to offer with words, a video is more convincing and this is what creates trust. Your viewers will feel as if they already know you once they watch the video. People are likely to buy from a brand that they can trust, which is better established through a video.

- Vides are more likely to go viral- videos are shared every day and if yours is a great video, you can be sure how many people you will reach out to without doing anything about it. People will learn about you from others sources just because you have a video in your marketing campaign, and this can determine the success of your marketing.

- Video sets you apart from the multitude- not everyone will be brave enough to include a video for their target market during online campaigns but only a few businesses, which are brave enough. This is what sets you apart from the rest. A video will help you stand out, which is just what you need in order to be well known for your brand, your products or services.

- It is much easier to understand a video than words- in case of a complex explanation a video will be easier to understand than a word explanation. It is easier to understand a concept when someone is demonstrating it than when it is just explained, therefore in case of a misunderstanding about your products or services, a video will favor you in that your prospects will understand you better in the end to trust what you are offering.

Chapter 4:
The Third and Fourth Strategy –
Interesting Diversification

There are many avenues for internet marketing that you can explore, and this is what is addressed in this section. Just like you would not place all your eggs in one basket when making an investment, you should also diversify your 'advertising portfolio' when marketing on the internet. This is the best way you can get excellent reach.

Make use of Various Platforms

A mistake many internet marketers do is to just rely on one search engine to reach their customers, and the most popular one is Google. Although Google holds onto first place firmly, it is losing its footing slightly as there are other platforms that have emerged and people are in those other platforms too. You should use Google but alongside those other platforms like Bing, Yahoo and AOL. Being well spread out can only mean that you will get better results.

In addition to these platforms, you can expand the type of internet marketing that you do so that you do not limit yourself. This means that you incorporate a holistic internet marketing plan as part of your strategy.

To begin with, you must have search engine optimization, so that when potential customers search using keywords that are related to your product offerings, they will find you and connect with you easily. Sponsoring search results is a form of search engine marketing and it ensures that when a certain keyword is entered, your product or service appears at the top of the list as you have paid for this service.

Social media optimization is another benefit you get from diversifying your efforts. This requires you to capitalize on a range of social media outlets as well as networks, so that you can increase your publicity as well as the amount of awareness for what you have to offer.

Then, you should also consider email marketing, which enables you to send a direct message to the consumer of your choice. As this approach makes it possible to be more personal, you are able to convert interest into sales more easily.

The point is that when you choose internet marketing, you must spread yourself across the internet as much as possible, and that is why you do not limit yourself to one platform. Consider what your typical customer uses the internet for in one day, and ensure that you establish your presence there.

There are other more direct means of interacting with your potential market and these can be used alongside Google and other platforms too in order to increase your chances of making it in the internet marketing.

Capitalize on social conversations

If you have been marketing in social networks, there is a lot that you can do in order to achieve more in internet market to reap its benefits. The good thing is that there are quite a number of social sites that you can take advantage of, with Twitter and Facebook taking the lead. To begin with, you need to ensure you have a certain amount of followers, which can easily be achieved using marketing on the social media and networking sites themselves. If you have already captured the attention of your so many followers, it is time to start engaging in social conversations for the purpose of marketing your brand.

Do not forget that every social site is different from the other and so, as you market your content always do it in a manner that is both entertaining and also native to the nature of the social site that you are using. It will benefit you to study a social site more closely before you start launching your campaign to ensure that you are doing the right thing.

Posting links to your content is an important marketing strategy to adopt but this should not be the only thing that you are doing, you need to engage them in a conversation, maybe by starting off with something interesting or funny, then follow it with a link to your content. Ensure that anything that you engage them in is something that really interests them so that they can follow the link that you have posted. When you have more people interacting with you, it becomes easier to spread the word and create a situation where their friends are attracted to your page and your product. It also ensures that you know first-hand what your customer is thinking and feeling, which allows you to make any necessary adjustments in quick time for the best results. Listening and responding will never fail you in social media marketing.

The reasons why social media platforms do not fail in internet marketing are:

a) It is the best way to establish trust with your clients-like I mentioned earlier, people are likely to buy from brands which they can fully trust. When you connect with people online, they are likely to start viewing your brand as something that they can trust and this is what triggers the intent to buy. You should be able to tell them the usefulness of your brand and after a few trials they will be ready to give it a try.

b) It is the best way to build your credibility- having so many followers in sites like Facebook and twitter can work in your advantage especially if these followers are interested in what you are selling. The people who are more likely to buy from your business are those that follow you in social media sites because you have established your credibility and they can tell that you are highly reliable. Aim to give them as much information as possible so that they will have full information pertaining to your brand for that time they will decide to place their orders.

c) It is very easy to enhance the image of your brand in social media sites- people in social sites are there to socialize and to learn about others. Take advantage of that to tell your story and to enhance your brand image so that people can connect to your brand more than before. This is the only place where people will get to know who you really are, where you started from and what you aim to achieve in the future. You should also aim to tell them what your plans for your clients are and how much more they can expect from your brand.

Chapter 5:
The Fifth and Sixth Strategies –
It's in the Information

Sites which have excellent, high quality content are more likely to have higher sales conversions than those sites that do not make the effort. That is a fact! When there is extensive competition in one field, you can stand out from the rest as a key strategy to generate profit. This section explains why information is ideal for internet marketing strategizing.

A Good Amount of Quality Content

Content is considered as king when it comes to internet marketing and there is never a situation where there is enough content. This is because people understand better what is being marketed by going through the content. If therefore you want to make a big name for yourself through internet marketing, you have to centralize content in your marketing strategy.

Keywords will make potential buyers find your website very easily in the search engines. This is what will drive a lot of traffic to your website. In the end, your website will get a good ranking in search engines like Google, making it visible to the millions of people that search for brands, products and services online. When there is traffic increasing to your site, more people are able to see what you have on offer. The more people, the higher the possibility that you will convert curious onlookers in buyers, and eventually, long term loyal customers.

Content has a lot to offer to internet marketing therefore consider partnering with the best content producers to make it in any online business. In as much as other things are considered important in marketing, content has a firm place at the top of the list.

Write an eBook

EBooks are more popular these days than ordinary books. Besides, books cost a lot of money since you will need to pay a publishing company as well as a distribution company for it to reach the intended readers. That is if you are publishing a book for your customers to read. However, an eBook will be much easier to work on. What you do is to come up with a good outline in your industry, which you are trying to solve with the products or services you are marketing. Create content that best suits you, but one that looks as if it is benefitting the readers more.

You do not want to make money through the eBook but to use it as a lead generation tool to what you are marketing. In the eBook, encourage readers to check out your website for further information on the issue and some of the solutions they might need. This will not cost you much since Amazon can allow you to upload an eBook for free. If you do not want it to become publicly available in this way, you can have it posted only on your website where customers can download it at will, or you can send it to those who are interested using a free link in email.

Should you make the decision to sell your eBook to potential customers, make the eBook affordable to the readers so that they can buy it. Before you know it, so many people would have read it and they are visiting your website to inquire more about the issue and the solutions. This will give your brand the popularity it needs to give you the success you deserve in the market. As you will also own all the intellectual property rights, you can use the eBook as a stepping stone into more publications, seminars and other written content resources that are available on your site.

Information about your brand will bring lots of benefits because:

- It gives your customers more reasons to stick around- if you have already stroked their interest in your brand, they will definitely be interested to know more about you and what you are offering. With the right content in place, they will have a good reason to stick around for a longer time and even to come back in order to read on. That is why more time should be spent in content creation because it offer consumers just what they need in order to make the final and most important decision.

- Content is what makes you highly visible in the search engines. What can you achieve without visibility in search engines? Online buyers search for what they are interested in and when you are highly ranked in search engines, you will be visible to the people who need what you are dealing with. That is why the right keywords should be used during content marketing. Include a few unique but strong keywords that will sell you and place you higher in the search engines so as to be seen easily by potential buyers.

- Information will increase traffic to your website- relevant and rich content will definitely bring in more consumers. This is the only way they will get to understand what you are selling so that they can make an informed decision thereafter. A great looking website without the content is always a failure; people will admire it but they will not buy because they do not know what you are selling. But good content will always bring in potential buyers to your website because they want to understand and your brand better and see what they can benefit from it. This increased traffic will benefit you in placing you higher in the search engines and this will make you more visible.

Chapter 6:
The Seventh and Eighth Strategies –
Social Mix and Mingling

When you want to market your product physically, you will find ways that you can mix and mingle with your potential clients, so that you are able to market what you have available in a setting that leaves them feeling comfortable and at ease. You can do the same as an internet marketer, and get excellent results in the process. All you need is to follow these two strategies.

Consider creating a LinkedIn group

LinkedIn is a great social site that connects professionals of all levels in one great platform. It is the best platform if you want to attract new business as an internet marketer. When you are on LinkedIn, and any other similar specialized social networking sites, customers tend to take what you have to say more seriously.

It is one of the best social sites to market yourself and what you are offering in the market. Creating a group in this social site will not cost you a dime, and it is very easy. The hard task will be in getting people into the group. Quality content and information that is relevant and dealing with current issues is guaranteed to get you followers. If they like your content, they it is possible they will share your page with their connections. Personal recommendations are highly appreciated, and have been proven to lead to increased traffic to a specific pate.

When you eventually get a good number of followers, you can use the group as a marketing platform, where you inform people indirectly what you deal with as you refer them to your website. Remember, the content is what will keep this group alive, so you should resist the temptation to pump out continuous marketing messages.

Use the group to engage in meaningful discussions about the issues at hand and why they should visit your site. You will be very lucky if you will be able to get a good number of people in the group who have interest in what you are dealing with. This is how one creates a professional network for their brand. This will also increase your exposure as a lot of people can share out what they learn form you to their other connections in the site and in other social sites.

Publish on niche blogs

If you are getting started in internet marketing, it will not be easy to make it on popular websites or in the front pages of popular online magazines and newspapers but you can use what you have to appear at least somewhere. There are popular niche blogs that would be willing to have your audience and many people who visit such blog sites will be able to connect with you. If you are lucky enough, you can be able to reach out to a few if not many potential customers.

In fact, it is probably better for you to gain a following from these niche blogs, and then establish your own blog later when you have good traction. You will learn what it takes to write an excellent article, and to have content that your customers will always find relevant.

What to do is to come up with a list of about 4 or 5 niche blogs that target the same market as you. Try to get in touch with the owners of the site and help them understand just how much importance you can bring to their blog sites if they agreed to publish you. Request to become a part of them as a guest blogger with a regular column for a fixed amount of time. This could be once a fortnight or once a month. You can for instance choose to offer some of what you are marketing for free to a few readers on their blog, which will work to benefit both of you. This will act as an added benefit that they can enjoy.

There is less competition in these blogs, therefore your brand will get full attention from potential buyers who visit these blogs. You can also build the loyalty of your brand slowly through such niche blogs, which can become something great eventually. Above all, you will get to save so much money on this marketing strategy and at the same time getting great results. Remember, you do not have to make a payment for being published as a guest author on a site, but SEO optimization and social media marketing are some of the avenues that will cost you.

Chapter 7:
The Ninth and Tenth Strategies –
The Old Favorites

Internet marketing has been around for some time, and the initial strategies that have been used have proven to be effective and timeless. Therefore, they should not be ignored simply because newer strategies are coming up. Instead, they should be reverted to and used to the best possible ability.

Do not ignore paid advertising

Paid advertising has so much to offer to online marketers that wants to get the most out of their tight budget. It is the best strategy to use if you want to specifically target people who are interested in what you are selling. It is a highly efficient strategy whose success can bring a lot of benefits to your marketing and business in general. Some of the benefits you get through paid search advertising are:

- You get to see immediate results

- You can take complete control of the marketing without fail

- It is the best strategy to test the success of your keywords as well as your campaign

You can choose to have pay per click advertising. This type of advertising means that you are not charged for people who simply see your advert. The only time that you have to make a payment is once a potential customer clicks on the advert of your product.

Give email marketing a shot

One thing that will not let you down in internet marketing is using more than one strategy to achieve the same results. Do not just rely on social network marketing but on email marketing as well. Social networks will always limit the amount of visibility that your brand will get and this means that you might not get the exact results that you are looking for. Search engines on the other hand have so many restrictions on websites that wants to be highly ranked. This will not work for you effectively as well.

If you combine those with email marketing, you might get tremendous results in the long run. You can come up with a PDF document with the content that you want to get out there to your target market, then send it to your created email list of potential customers. You can also send it as an eBook that they can download and go through whatever it is that you are marketing.

Email marketing is great as it is less costly, it will target people that are already interested in your brand, it gives potential buyers a call for action which can work to your advantage and you can easily do a follow up to see how successful the strategy was.

Chapter 8:
Mistakes to Avoid in Internet Marketing

Just as it is easy to become an expert in internet marketing with the right motivation and guidance, you can easily make mistakes along the way. This can cost you so much money and kill your dream of ever becoming a guru and enjoying all the benefits that come with it. It is important to know some of the mistakes that internet marketers make every day so that you can be on the lookout as you work to achieve your goals. Understand that even the best marketers in the world make mistakes at one time or another, therefore once it happens, do not beat yourself up. The sign of a sure winner is someone that is willing to pick themselves up and move forward, no matter what they are facing. Some of the mistakes to look out for are as below:

Targeting just anyone

Every marketer should have a specific target in mind, where they focus whenever they are marketing. You do not market to anyone but to a specific kind of group. What you should do in the beginning is to identify your target group. You need to know how they shop, where they shop and what interests them the most, then you know what strategies you will use in order to reach out to them. You will waste so much resources if you will market to everyone else and you might not be getting the expected results in the end. With the target in mind, choosing the strategies to use in your marketing campaign becomes very easy.

Procrastinating

This happens all the time especially if you are really not up to the task. Many new internet marketers do not get everything done when it should be done because they keep pushing it to the future. If you want to succeed in internet marketing, everything has to fall in place at the right time. This means that you have to do what you have to do every time. There is no room for postponing if you really want to enjoy success in the long run. With so much work to do, you need a plan that you can follow through without fail. Motivate yourself and work with a serious group to accomplish all the goals on the right time.

So Much Information at a Go

Getting started in internet marketing is exciting enough and what many people do is to gather as much information as they can get especially over the internet and in books. This is not bad at all, but you are likely to get overwhelmed by so much information, which could be hard to digest and thereafter put into practice. Learning is important but you have to learn bit by bit as you put what you learn in practice. Do not be in a hurry to learn so much at once if you want to enjoy internet marketing and achieve success in it. Information will always be there and new information keeps coming up every day. You need to learn little by little to get it right and to be able to apply only what you feel is right at a particular stage of your campaign.

Unrealistic Goals

Setting goals is a good thing so as to know how much you are achieving at the end of each promotion or campaign. However, you have to make sure that your goals are meaningful and attainable. Unrealistic goals are the killers of many dreams all over the world. When one realizes that they cannot meet their goals, they lose hope and that dream dies a permanent death. In internet marketing, you have to chase the true numbers and not numbers that you know very well are unachievable. Always set goals that measure up to your campaign and you will be happy with the little progress that you make every day. When this is done consistently as you increase your campaign pace, you will enjoy great results. Do not focus higher when you can go up step by step, a little at a time.

Missing Out on a Chance to Test Your Ideas

Internet marketing is very good and it gives marketers a chance to test their ideas every time they want to. This way, you can figure out if you are on the best line or not and you can change the tactic if the idea did not work as expected. However, many people are in a rush to get everything done that they do not take some time off to test their ideas. This is a mistake that can affect your campaign. If you want to be a good marketer, cut to the chase and take time to test everything that you build.

Ignoring Web Analytics

It is always good to find out how much you are achieving through your internet marketing campaigns from time to time so that you will know what to expect in the end. Some business people ignore this completely even when they have been presented with several tools through which they can measure the progress of their marketing. Such tools as Google Analytics for instance can easily tell you how many people have visited your website. This information can tell you if you are doing it right or if there is need for some changes and improvements so as to achieve the desired results. You can also tell how your website visitors got there and what they did in your website. It is important to know what is happening in your website at all times so that you will know if your marketing campaign is working as it should or it is not giving you the results that you were anticipating. Ignoring the web analytics will keep you in the dark and you may never know whether you are making progress or you are just doing all the campaigns for no results. Instead of waiting for failed result in the end, check out the analytics from time to time and make changes toward what you want to get on time.

Conclusion

Consumers these days are more interested in shopping for products and services online than ever before. It offers so much convenience and this is what internet marketers should capitalize on. Companies have now started their internet marketing campaigns and they are succeeding in getting the attention they need for their brands. This is because there is a lot to gain and a little to lose if you gave internet marketing a chance and chances of making it big in this kind of campaign are very high.

Are you ready to give internet marketing a chance and become the internet marketing guru that you have always dreamt of becoming? You have to get started and face the challenges head on if you want to enjoy the amazing results that come in the end. This eBook has all the strategies that you need to get you started and take you to a place where you can start enjoying great rewards.

Once you kick off your campaign, you can have a user polls section somewhere in your website where your visitors can tell you what they think about your website and the campaign in general. Always remember that your user opinions are very important. You can learn so much from them since they are the ones on the receiving end. This will help you to make any changes if it will be necessary and you can enjoy the success of the campaign thereafter.

One thing you should never forget is that using more than one advertising method will never fail you. If possible, use all ten strategies!! It will in fact increase your chances of becoming a success in this business.

www.ingramcontent.com/pod-product-compliance
Lightning Source LLC
Chambersburg PA
CBHW070430190526
45169CB00003B/1484